MONSTERS
WENDIGO

BY Q.L. PEARCE

KIDHAVEN PRESS
A part of Gale, Cengage Learning

GALE
CENGAGE Learning™

Detroit • New York • San Francisco • New Haven, Conn • Waterville, Maine • London

LIBRARY OF CONGRESS CATALOGING-IN-PUBLICATION DATA

Pearce, Q. L. (Querida Lee)
  Wendigo / by Q.L. Pearce.
     p. cm. – (Monsters)
  Includes bibliographical references and index.
  ISBN 978-0-7377-4409-5 (hardcover)
  1. Windigos–Juvenile literature. 2. Algonquin Indians–Folklore–Juvenile literature. I. Title. II. Title: Windigo.
  E99.A35P43 2009
  971.3004'9733–dc22

2008052916

KidHaven Press
27500 Drake Rd.
Farmington Hills, MI 48331

ISBN-13: 978-0-7377-4409-5
ISBN-10: 0-7377-4409-X

Printed in the United States of America
1 2 3 4 5 6 7 13 12 11 10 09

CONTENTS

Chapter 1

The Spirit of Lonely Places

In a freezing, winter landscape in the Great Lakes region of North America, a young Ojibwa hunter is making his way home through the snow. Darkness has come early and shadows loom within the dense pine forest. The winter has been harsh and he has found little game to feed his family. They will have to make do with what is left of the wild rice they have stored in baskets. He can see his home ahead. The **wigwam** is covered with birch bark. Smoke rises through a hole in the roof signaling that there is a warm fire inside.

Something in the nearby woods moves. He stops

to listen. A soft hissing sound echoes through the trees. Is it the wind? The hair rises on the back of the man's neck. It could be an animal, but it might be something else. The man remembers the stories he has heard of a monster more terrible than death itself. He turns to run as fast as the heavy snow will allow. The young man grips his knife and races to the safety of his wigwam. Once inside he huddles with his family. He has dropped his knife outside but he will wait until the light of day to search for it. Something else might be out there. Hidden by the falling snow, a wendigo may be searching for a meal.

A Fearful Sight

The wendigo is part of the **folklore** of the Algonquin people in the northern United States and Canada, including the Ojibwa, Cree, Innu, Abenaki, Blackfoot, and Mik'maq. Each of these groups has its own version of the monster's name such as chenoo, kewohqu, wheetigo, and windikouk. The name most commonly used in modern American society is wendigo, or wendigowak for more than one. Some tribes claim that it is an evil spirit that can possess the body of an unsuspecting human. Others say that a wendigo was once human. There are many descriptions of the monster. It may be a version of **Bigfoot** or a cross between Bigfoot, a **werewolf**, and a **troll**. A wendigo may have glowing eyes set deep in the sockets, long,

uneven yellowed fangs, and a very long tongue. Its thin, ragged lips are always bloody and do not cover the teeth. The heart of the wendigo is a solid block of ice visible beneath the creature's **translucent** skin.

Most have yellowish or gray skin that may or may not be matted with mangy hair. They smell of decay and rot. Tall and long-limbed, the body is **gaunt**, deformed, and missing toes. Some say a wendigo is so thin that when it turns sideways it disappears, but wherever it goes it leaves bloody footprints. Some say that all of these descriptions are correct because some wendigowak are also **shapeshifters**.

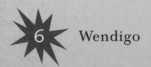

The wendigo lives alone in the forest, and feeds on the flesh of humans.

The wendigo lives alone in the forest, feeding on the flesh of travelers. The monster moves among the trees, tracking its prey silently, just out of sight. It hunts at dawn and dusk, but often waits until night to eat its victim. Sometimes it traps and stores its living victims in caves, or stockpiles flesh high in the trees.

The more human flesh a wendigo eats the larger the beast grows. Its appetite grows, too. Because of this the creature is always gorging itself, but it is also always starving and never satisfied. When it cannot find its preferred food of human flesh it will eat rotten wood, slimy swamp moss, and mushrooms.

Becoming a Wendigo

According to legend, wendigowak usually start out as human beings. There are several ways the transformation can happen. The most common cause of the horrible change is **cannibalism**. In the dead of winter, food can sometimes be scarce or even unavailable. Although it is rare, a person driven mad with hunger might choose to save himself by eating human flesh. Legend says this gives an evil spirit the opportunity to take over the person's body and turn him into a monster.

Some say that the bite of a wendigo may also cause the change to take place. An innocent victim might fight off the monster and avoid becoming a meal, only to be infected with horrible cravings for human flesh. In fact, regular food can make

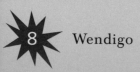

The wendigo lives alone in the forest, moving among the trees, tracking its prey.

the victim vomit. In the early stages, the new half human-half wendigo is very dangerous because it still looks like a person and can attack unsuspecting friends or family members.

Another version of the legend says that a wendigo can slowly transform a sleeping person. While the human is dreaming, a wendigo spirit calls his or her name over and over, slowly infecting the dreamer with what is called *the fever*. With each passing day the prey becomes more vicious and obsessed with thoughts of eating human flesh. The nightmares get worse until the victim is driven insane and runs into the forest where the hungry wendigo is waiting.

The final way that a human being may turn into a wendigo is to be cursed by a **shaman** or to willingly participate in a magical **ritual** to bring about the change. The transformation takes place a little at a time. Nightmares make the person who is turning into a wendigo afraid to sleep, and when they are awake they may be calm one moment then crying hysterically the next. At first their senses grow sharper, particularly the sense of smell. The soles of the feet become sore and painful so a victim refuses to wear shoes. At last a frigid crystal spreads within the person's chest turning the heart to ice. The coldness expands until everything human disappears and only the monster remains.

DEFEATING THE WENDIGO

Most people who believe the legend of the wendigo say that the beast is nearly impossible to kill because it can heal its wounds instantly. Even so, a few claim that the creature has a weakness. An Ojibwa medicine man named Big Goose was once famous for destroying a wendigo, but he did

When a wendigo cannot find human flesh to eat, it sometimes will eat mushrooms.

not work alone. He had the help of a **Manitou**, or magical spirit, who changed him into a mighty giant named Missahba. Because of his size and strength, Big Goose was able to battle and defeat the wendigo then return to his human form.

For those who cannot use magic to kill the beast, its icy heart may be cracked and broken by a silver stake, or silver-tipped arrow. Killing the monster is

The Spirit of Lonely Places

only the first step. To be certain that it will not come back to life, the slayer must use a silver axe to chop up the body starting with the head. Next the head must be burned and the heart buried in a silver box. Any remaining body parts should be hidden separately in a variety of **remote** locations. Another possibility is to trap the wendigo and expose it to a raging fire so that its heart melts. Afterwards legend says the body must be cut up and buried.

A shaman may try to cure a newly transformed wendigo, but the remedy is rarely successful. The medicine man has to prepare a vat of boiling fat. Next he must trick the monster into opening its mouth so he can pour the fat down its throat. If the treatment works, the wendigo throws up its frozen heart and returns to its human form.

Chapter 2

Whispers and Warnings

The Algonquin tribes did not write down stories about the wendigo. They whispered the tales around the campfire and passed the stories from generation to generation. The first known written account of this legendary creature is from the seventeenth century. Father Paul Le Jeune was a French Jesuit missionary. In 1632 he went to Quebec, Canada, to establish missions and Christian villages for the Native Americans. Father Paul regularly sent detailed reports to his superiors.

In 1636, the priest sent a message to say that he was worried about something that had happened in a small village. A few weeks earlier a native woman had gone into a **trance**. When she recovered, she warned the residents that a wendigo was nearby. Although he had not seen it himself, Father Paul wrote about the beast, describing it as something like a werewolf. The legend of the werewolf was well known in Europe and would be easy for his superiors to understand.

A North American Appearance

Father Paul explained that he was not frightened for himself. He was more concerned that the other villagers were afraid. He felt they might ignore his Christian teachings and return to old **superstitions**. There is no official record of any wendigo attacks during Father Paul's stay in Canada, and in 1649 he returned to France.

It was more than one hundred years before another European wrote about the monster. The Hudson's Bay Company was a trading company established in Canada in 1670. The group set up a series of trading posts where they could bargain with Native Americans for furs. James Isham was a Hudson's Bay Company employee who lived in Manitoba, Canada, from 1743 to 1749.

Like Father Paul, Isham kept careful notes about what he saw and heard while he lived among the Indians. He eventually published his notes as *Observations of Hudson's Bay*. He wrote that the Indians warned him to be careful of a creature called Whit-ti-co that sounded to him like some sort of

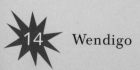

A Native American couple exchanges furs for a rifle at a Hudson's Bay Company trading post in Canada in the late 17th century. Native Americans reported sightings of the wendigo in the area.

President Theodore Roosevelt (center) visits Yellowstone National Park in 1903. In Roosevelt's book "Wilderness Hunter," he discussed the story of a trapper who encountered a wendigo.

devil. It is more likely that the monster they described was a wendigo.

THE PRESIDENT'S STORY

Wendigo sightings have been reported in Wisconsin, Michigan, Ohio, and as far west as North Dakota and Montana. A branch of the Ojibwa settled on the plains of Montana and the legend of the wendigo traveled with them. Before he became president of the United States in 1901, Theodore Roosevelt wrote a book called *Wilderness Hunter*. It was published in 1892. He included a story he had been told by an old,

grey-haired trapper named Bauman. Some readers think the story was about an encounter with Bigfoot. Others think that the creature was a wendigo. Roosevelt noted that although decades had passed

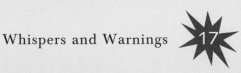

Whispers and Warnings

since the actual event happened, the trapper shivered with dread when he related the tale.

It seems that Bauman and a friend were trapping beaver not far from the Salmon River between Idaho and Montana. They decided to hunt in a small valley that most people avoided because of its fearsome **reputation**. A year before Bauman arrived **prospectors** had found the half-eaten body of a man in the same valley.

The men had to hike in on foot and they set up camp. The next day they spent many hours setting traps. When they returned, their camp had been torn apart and there were many large footprints on the ground. The trappers gathered up their scattered supplies, then built a huge fire and slept near it. Bauman told Roosevelt that he had heard something large moving in the woods that night making a harsh moaning sound. He had also smelled a foul beastly odor and had seen a huge shadow looming close by. Whatever it was seemed to fear the fire.

The next morning the men decided to pick up their traps and leave. Near the end of the day there were only a few traps left to recover, but the sun was setting. The men agreed to save time by splitting up. Bauman continued to retrieve the traps while his friend went to the camp to pack their gear. When Bauman finally returned to camp the fire had gone out and the campsite was dark. He called out to his friend but there was no answer. A moment later he found out why. His friend's dead

body was stretched out near a fallen tree trunk. His neck was broken and there were four deep fang marks in his throat. Terrified, Bauman took nothing but a rifle and raced down the hill. When he finally made his way back to the nearest village, the residents said that his friend had been the victim of a wendigo.

When commenting on the story in his book, Theodore Roosevelt said that the animal-like footprints at the camp sounded like those of a black bear or a cougar. He suggested that a large cougar might have attacked Bauman's friend. Trappers familiar with the tale disagreed. They pointed out that a wendigo often shared its territory with other predators, so a bear or a cougar may have visited the camp, but it was a wendigo that made the kill.

The Far North

Rumors of wendigowak sightings are not uncommon in Ontario, Canada. In 1940, the area experienced a terrible famine due to three harsh winters in a row. Near the town of Kenora, which was once known as Rat Portage, hunters and trappers often spent days or even weeks alone in the woods. A few claimed to see or feel a wendigo nearby. Some said it had the giant head of a deer or the head of a wolf, and that it could walk across water without sinking. Even today, locals warn tourists who visit nearby Lake Mameigwess to be watchful, particularly near the Cave of the Wendigo. According to legend,

In 1934, the Royal Canadian Mounted Police were called to the scene of a trapper's base camp, similar to the one illustrated here, in Manitoba, where they found a man tied up by his companions because he had been taken over by a wendigo.

hikers and hunters who become lost may be drawn in by **hallucinations** that lure them to within striking distance of a wendigo. Monster sightings around Kenora have continued into the twenty-first century, earning the town the title "Wendigo Capitol of the World."

On an icy January afternoon in 1934, in the Canadian province of Manitoba, the Royal Canadian Mounted Police received an emergency report. At a trapper's base camp near the small settlements of Burntwood Bay and Reindeer Lake, a man was tied to a sled outside in the freezing cold. Sergeant Percy Rose raced to the site by dogsled to save the man before he froze to death. Rose was stunned to find that the man's terrified coworkers were close by but they refused to help. In fact, they told the officer that they had tied the man to the sled themselves because he had suddenly become very violent. The frightened trappers thought that the man had been taken over by a wendigo. Although a local newspaper was said to have reported the incident, the article did not say what eventually happened to the victim.

Residents of Cobalt, Ontario, are so familiar with the tales of the beast that they have a **nickname** for it. They call it *Old Yellow Top* because of the color of its skin or its mangy fur. The latest sighting in that area was in 1997. A trucker driving near the town of St. Catharines, Ontario, not far from Niagara Falls, told authorities that he saw

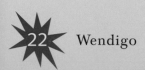

the creature near the road. Sightings have been reported in eastern North America as well, from the heavily forested mountains south of Quebec along the St. John River in New Brunswick, and into the wild backcountry of Maine.

CHAPTER 3

TRADITION AND LAW

In most cultures, certain acts or behaviors are never allowed. Among the people of the Algonquian tribes, and in most cultures, cannibalism is forbidden even if a person is starving to death. Scientists who study Native American culture think that the legend of the wendigo was created to make people afraid of eating human flesh. In the dead of winter when supplies ran out, people believed that even a mouthful could cause them to become a wendigo. That meant they would transform into a monster, cursed to live a lonely life, feared and hated by all. For most it was a fate worse than starving to death.

The wendigo's **voracious** appetite that could

never be satisfied was a warning against eating or drinking too much. This aspect of the legend may have been designed to reduce greedy behavior like hoarding food. In times of famine people were encouraged to share and help each other as much as possible to keep everyone out of the clutches of the wendigo. Parents used stories of the wendigo to keep children from wandering too far from home at night or during winter.

MONSTER MADNESS

By the end of the 19th century, medical doctors started to have Native American patients who claimed to be under the control of an evil wendigo spirit. At first the doctors believed that there was nothing wrong and the patients were making up their symptoms. Then a pattern began to show. Symptoms appeared to start after a famine. Some of the patients had spent a lot of time alone in the wilderness.

Native Americans who were suffering seemed to be depressed and frightened. They would lose the desire to eat normal food, but confessed to craving human flesh. Sometimes they would become violent. The Indians acted much like patients in Europe who believed they were becoming werewolves. All of the victims believed that the wendigo myth was true. They were all sure they had the fever. Doctors decided that the problem was a mental illness. They even came up with a name for

Indians sometimes behaved like patients in Europe who believed they were werewolves (pictured). These victims believed the wendigo myth was true.

the condition. They called it Wendigo **psychosis** (also spelled Windigo and Witiko).

Sometimes a sufferer went to see a shaman who would try to cure the victim by pouring hot fat down his or her throat. Some people were "cured."

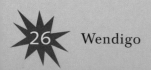

Others still had symptoms. A few were considered dangerous and were cruelly executed. Accounts of such executions can be found in the diaries and letters of travelers.

TALES OF HORROR

Major H. Long was a scout for the United States Army in 1823. When he retired he wrote a **memoir** that included a tragic story. When he visited a camp near Lake of the Woods in Ontario, residents told Long a frightening story. A group of about forty people had camped in the area in 1811 during a season of terrible food shortages. When a few people died of starvation, the survivors chose to eat the flesh of the dead. By the time help arrived only one woman remained. The evidence showed that she had killed her own husband and children. Although Long did not record the method, he notes that the woman was immediately executed.

In 1859, Scottish nobleman James Carnegie began a yearlong trek through the Canadian province of Saskatchewan. On his travels he kept a diary. One of the entries was about the execution of a man of the Salteaux tribe. The victim had been acting strangely. He stopped speaking and had not eaten for over a month. His neighbors were afraid that the man was becoming a wendigo. According to Carnegie's notes, the man was struck down by a member of the tribe and buried alive. Hours later

An Indian shaman would try to cure a wendigo victim by pouring hot fat down his or her throat.

28   Wendigo

they dug him up and burned his body until there was nothing left but ashes.

Another eyewitness account is credited to a Scottish fur trader, but the writer's name has been lost to history. It concerned a man who visited a small outpost near Trout Lake in Alberta, Canada, in 1896. At first the visitor complained of strange dreams. He said that while he slept a horrible creature came to him. The nightmares finally drove him mad and he became violent. The writer of the account noted that the victim seemed barely human. At first the frightened residents locked the man in a cabin, and then they killed him and buried the body. Believing that he had become a wendigo, they rolled heavy logs over the grave to prevent the body from escaping if it came back to life.

A Tragic Mistake

Fear of a wendigo has often led to tragedy. The December 7, 1986, edition of the *Winnipeg Free Press* carried a story about a court case in Rat Portage, Ontario. Weeks before, rumors of a wendigo nearby had frightened the local residents. To protect their families, community leaders formed groups to guard the town day and night. About a week later a young guard was at his post when he saw a figure running. Terrified, he shot at the distant form. Sadly, he had actually shot and killed his own foster father. During the trial the defense suggested that the guard's father had left his post and was running back to it when he had been killed. The young guard was found guilty of the crime, but everyone knew that he thought he was shooting at a wendigo, not a human. The guard was sentenced to only six months of hard labor.

THE TRIALS

Native American acceptance of the wendigo legend finally became a legal problem. Was cannibalism a sign of mental illness? If someone believed an evil spirit possessed him or her, were they responsible for their own actions? The winter of 1878 was severe in Alberta, Canada. Swift Runner was a Cree trapper who lived with his wife, six children, his mother, and his brother. As food supplies ran out, Swift Runner grew more and more desperate. When his eldest son died of starvation, the trapper's grip on reality shattered. He killed his entire family and fed on their flesh. When he realized what he had done, Swift Runner surrendered to authorities. He was given a medical examination and doctors agreed that he was suffering from wendigo psychosis and was mentally unstable. After a brief trial he was sentenced to death and executed at Fort Saskatchewan.

Sometimes tribal leaders took the law into their own hands. That was the case in 1907 of an eighty-seven-year-old Cree Indian known as Jack Fiddler who lived near Island Lake, Ontario. He was an *ogimaa,* meaning chief and a shaman, known for his

On a year-long trip to Saskatchewan, Scottish nobleman James Carnegie included an entry in his diary that described the execution of a man whom tribal members believed was becoming a wendigo.

skill at defeating wendigowak. This often meant killing people who were possessed by the monster. The list included one of his brothers, Peter, who ran out of food during a trading expedition and reportedly turned into a wendigo.

When the Canadian authorities heard that Jack had killed some fourteen people, they arrested him and his brother, Joseph. The men were charged with the murder of Joseph's daughter-in-law. Jack escaped and hung himself from a tree. During

Joseph's trial, an eyewitness explained that the woman had been in terrible pain and her death was an act of mercy. Others argued that the Indians knew nothing of Canadian law. They had acted according to their own customs, which allowed the killing of a wendigo.

Although local missionaries and traders of the Hudson's Bay Company tried to save his life, Joseph was convicted of murder and executed in 1909. Sadly, his sentence was overturned, but not until three days after his death.

Chapter 4

Wendigo Reborn

The wendigo has long been an evil, terrifying creature in Native American culture. For those who hear its cry, it is a warning. For the poor traveler who sees one, it is a death sentence. In modern American culture the monster has found a new place as a frightening character in books and movies and even in video games. The wendigo's dreadful appearance and hair-raising deeds make it a perfect character for fans of horror.

Between the Pages

One of the earliest and best known books about the creature is Algernon Blackwood's 1910 **novella**, *The Wendigo*. Blackwood was an English writer

Ghost story writer Algernon Blackwood published a novella titled The Wendigo in 1910.

who once lived in Canada. He based his story on an event that was rumored to be true. The book has plenty of creepy details about the wendigo including how it stalks its prey, the chilling sound it makes, and how it drives its victim insane. The interesting thing about this story is that the monster does not make an actual appearance. The slow, terrible changes to the victim are the center of the tale.

Unlike in Blackwood's book, the wendigo in Stephen King's horror novel *Pet Sematary* does not stay true to the legend. Published in 1983, the story is about a family with two children who move to Maine. The father, Louis, learns that there is a graveyard near their home. When the family cat is killed, a neighbor shows him a hidden part of the graveyard where Mik'maq Indians buried victims of cannibalism. The characters do not know that the burial ground is haunted by a wendigo. When Louis buries the cat there, the animal returns to life as a frightening version of the pet. When his young son dies, Louis makes the huge mistake of digging up his body and burying him in the soil of the old graveyard. The result is very disturbing.

Just for Kids

Most school libraries have at least one copy of *Scary Stories to Tell in the Dark* by Alvin Schwartz (1986). It is a collection of retellings, myths, folk-

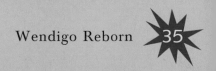

lore, and urban legends. The book includes a tale called "The Wendigo." It is very short and similar to the classic account by Algernon Blackwood. A reference to the victim's fiery, burning feet and other details are from the original story.

Another children's book of scary short stories, *Giant Short & Shivery*, by Robert San Souci (1999) includes a short story about a group of sailors and their mean-tempered captain. They land on an island where a young boy warns them that there is something in the trees watching them. It turns out to be a wendigo.

Fans of poetry will find the wendigo in two very different poems. Canadian author, historian, and poet George Harry Bowering wrote an eerie poem called "Windigo." The work describes the creature's hard ice heart and huge eyes rolling in bloody sockets. American poet Ogden Nash took a more humorous approach in his poem, "The Wendigo." To describe the monster he used words such as blubbery, sucky, leathery, slimy, and rubbery. He also notes that the wendigo has tentacles.

COMICS

Many young readers love comic books. Fans of Marvel Comics may be familiar with the villain, Wendigo, an enemy of the Hulk. The Wendigo first appeared in the Incredible Hulk #162, April 1973, under the title of *Spawn of the Flesh-Eater.*

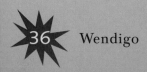

One of the enemies of the Incredible Hulk (pictured at a comic strip convention) is Wendigo.

The character, whose real name is Paul Cartier, has white fur, sharp claws, a long tail, superhuman strength, and incredible endurance. Unfortunately for the creature it is not very smart. The spirit of the Wendigo character can also move from one person to another. The human left behind does not remember what he did while he was possessed. Other Marvel heroes who have faced Wendigo are X-Men, Spiderman, Captain Marvel, and Wolverine.

The Big Screen

Wendigowak are well represented in horror and fantasy films. They are sometimes shown as skeletal creatures with bare sagging skin and huge eyes. Others look more like the legendary Bigfoot. The first film to introduce the cannibal spirit of the Algonquin was *The Lure of the Windigo*. It was a silent film released in 1914. It is about a young married woman living in the wilds of Canada with her husband. A Canadian Mountie lures her away from her husband and abandons her. A Native American friend helps her to reunite with her husband and then finds a frightening way to settle the score with the Mountie.

The list of films that feature the evil spirit is long and it includes *The Wendigo* (1940), *Ravenous* (1999), *Frostbiter: Wrath of the Wendigo* (1996), and *An American Wendigo in London* (1989). The films *Ginger Snaps* (2000), *Ginger Snaps Back* (2004), and *Ginger Snaps:*

Unleashed (2004) are actually about werewolves, but the curse originates with a wendigo. One thing that many of these films have in common is that they are frightening and very gory.

PRIME TIME

As the wendigo legend became more familiar to readers and movie goers it was only a matter of time before the creature showed up on the small screen. The creature appears as a villain in such series as *X-Files*, *Charmed*, and *Supernatural*.

In "Detour," *X-Files* Season 5 (1997), the main characters, Scully and Mulder, are on their way to an FBI meeting. A detour leads them through a wooded area where an invisible being is spiriting people away. The creature has many traits of the wendigo.

Charmed is a show about three sisters who happen to be witches. "Wendigo" is the 12th episode in Season 1 (1999). One of the sisters, Piper, is attacked by a wendigo disguised as an FBI agent. A bite turns Piper into a wendigo herself, complete with the fever and icy heart. The monster takes human form during the day. At night it takes its natural form and feeds on human hearts.

The most recent series to include the creature is *Supernatural*. Two brothers, Sam and Dean, work together to defeat supernatural beings, from ghosts to demons. "Wendigo," the second episode in Season 1, aired in 2005. After meeting two teens who

Actor Roy Campsall as Wendigo in the TV series Supernatural.

are looking for a missing brother, Sam and Dean learn that several people have disappeared. The creature responsible is a wendigo, but it has an unusual ability to speak and **mimic** people's voices. The brothers must find a way to overcome the monster and perhaps save some of its victims.

IN NAME ONLY

The wendigo has made a name for itself in modern culture, in books, movies, and on television. The Algonquin spirit has also lent its name to natural sites in North America such as Windigo National Park in Michigan, Lake Windigo in northern Min-

Windigo is the name of one of the visitor centers at Michigan's Isle Royale National Park.

nesota, and Wendigo Lake and Camp Wendigo in Ontario, Canada. Tourists and sport enthusiasts flock to such places in spring, summer, and even fall. To most visitors the wendigo is just a fictional character, a myth, a story to tell around the campfire.

But in winter, when the long nights are cold and dark, and the tourists are gone, it is easier to believe in the old stories. When the land is harsh and unforgiving, those who remain stay inside at night and lock their doors. Then it is not too hard to imagine that a wendigo may be out there somewhere in the dark lonely places.

Glossary

Bigfoot: A legendary humanlike ape creature living in the American Northwest.

cannibalism: The eating of human flesh by another human.

folklore: Traditional stories of a group culture or country.

gaunt: Very thin and bony.

hallucinations: The illusion of hearing, feeling, or seeing something that is not there.

Manitou: A guardian spirit that may be good or evil.

memoir: A personal story or record of one's life.

mimic: To imitate or copy someone's appearance or voice.

nickname: A pet name or invented name.

novella: A written work that is longer than a short story and shorter than a novel.

prospectors: Someone who searches for mineral deposits such as gold or silver.

psychosis: A mental disorder, a distorted perception of reality.

remote: Distant from civilization, isolated.

reputation: The accepted opinion about a person or place.

ritual: A regular pattern or set of procedures.

shaman: A person who can go between the physical and spiritual worlds; a person who may have healing powers or can see the future.

shapeshifters: Beings who can change from one physical form to another.

superstitions: Illogical beliefs in a being or the power of an object, place, or action.

trance: A dreamlike or semi-unconscious state in which someone is unaware of the environment around them.

translucent: Sheer or semitransparent.

troll: A mythical cave-dwelling being who is large, strong, ugly, and not very smart.

voracious: Extremely hungry or greedy for something such as food.

werewolf: A legendary creature that is half human-half wolf.

wigwam: A Native American dwelling usually made of poles and bark or woven materials.

FOR FURTHER EXPLORATION

BOOKS

Algernon Blackwood, *The Wendigo*. Rockville, MD: Wildside Press, 2002. The classic wendigo novella by a master horror writer. The book has large print to make it easier to read when sitting around a campfire.

Basil Johnston, *The Manitous: Supernatural World of the Ojibway*. New York: Harper Perennial, 1996. A collection of traditional tales of Manitous and monsters of the Ojibwa people. Although this book is written for adults, young readers will enjoy the simple stories that are based in oral tradition.

Alvin Schwartz, *Scary Stories to Tell in the Dark*, 25th Anniversary Edition. New York: HarperTrophy, 1986. A supersized collection of short stories, folktales, urban legends, and myths. Some are scarier than others, but there is something for everyone. Includes the story of the wendigo.

WEB SITES

All Things Wendigo (http://www.thewendigo
.com/flash/links.html). A collection of history
and facts about the wendigo. Also includes infor-
mation on films, books, and television.

Scary for Kids (http://www.scaryforkids.com/).
A fun site that includes mazes, scary flash games,
stories, and much more.

INDEX

Picture Credits

About the Author

Q. L. Pearce has written more than 100 trade books for children, and more than 30 classroom workbooks and teacher manuals on the topics of reading, science, math, and values. Pearce has written science-related articles for magazines; regularly gives presentations at schools, bookstores, and libraries; and is a frequent contributor to the educational program of the Los Angeles County Fair. She is the Assistant Regional Advisor for the Society of Children's Book Writers and Illustrators in Orange, San Bernardino, California.